W9-BXS-561

LIFEWATCH

The Mystery of Nature

CUB TO GRIZZLY BEAR

Oliver S. Owen

Published by Abdo & Daughters, 4940 Viking Drive, Suite 622, Edina, Minnesota 55435.

Copyright © 1996 by Abdo Consulting Group, Inc., Pentagon Tower, P.O. Box 36036, Minneapolis, Minnesota 55435 USA. International copyrights reserved in all countries. No part of this book may be reproduced in any form without written permission from the publisher.

Printed in the United States.

Cover Photo credit: Peter Arnold, Inc.
Interior Photo credits: Peter Arnold, Inc.

Edited by Bob Italia

Library of Congress Cataloging-in-Publication Data

Owen, Oliver S., 1920
Pup to grizzly bear / Oliver S. Owen.
    p. cm. — (Lifewatch)
Includes bibliographical references (p.31) and index.
ISBN 1-56239-486-X
1. Grizzly bear—Juvenile literature. [1. Grizzly bear. 2. Bears.] I. Title. II. Series: Owen, Oliver S., 1920 Lifewatch.
QL737.C27O94 1995
599.74'446—dc20
                                    95-3317
                                        CIP
                                        AC

Contents

The Grizzly Bear

The grizzly bear is one of the largest and strongest carnivores on Earth. It belongs to the same species as the Alaskan brown bear.

The grizzly is found in the mountains of Idaho, Montana, Wyoming, and western Canada. It weighs up to 800 pounds (363 kg) and may be eight feet (2.5 m) long. The larger brown bear weighs up to 1,700 pounds (771 kg) and may be nine feet (2.7 m) long. The grizzly has long hair on the back which is tipped with white. This gives it a "grizzled" look. That's how it got the name "grizzly."

The grizzly has powerful jaws. Its teeth are designed to tear and grind flesh. It cannot see very well. Although it has short ears it has good hearing. The grizzly also has an excellent sense of smell. It probably smells its prey before it sees it.

All grizzlies have a distinctive "hump" behind the neck which sets them apart from the black bear. The toes are long, strong and tipped with curved, sharply-pointed nails.

Notice the strong, sharply curved claws on this grizzly bear.

Animals like dogs and cats walk on their toes. But not the grizzly. The sole of the grizzly's foot is flat. It leaves a footprint like that of humans. In 1983, a 17-year-old grizzly was trapped in Yellowstone National Park. This 700-pound (318-kg) male left a footprint which was almost 12 inches (30 cm) long!

Grizzlies are not usually dangerous. However, if they are surprised, very hungry, or wounded, they may attack humans.

The grizzly bear and brown bear have captured the interest of people the world over. They appear on the coat of arms of many nations. The city of Berne, Switzerland, and Berlin, Germany, were named after them. California's state emblem is the Great Golden Bear. It honors the thousands of grizzlies that once lived there. The University of California football and basketball teams are called the "Bears." For many Americans, the grizzly has been a symbol of both determination and power.

CALIFORNIA REPUBLIC

Vanishing Bears

Early in the last century there were about 100,000 grizzly bears living in the lower United States. Today there are less than 1,000. (However, about 12,000 grizzlies live in Alaska and 16,000 in western Canada.) The advance of civilization caused this serious drop in numbers.

In the 1800s, white settlers invaded grizzly country. Many were sheep and cattle ranchers. Sometimes a grizzly would kill a lamb or a sick cow. Soon these settlers declared war on all grizzlies, whether they were killing livestock or not.

The grizzlies had other problems. Loggers were destroying their natural living areas. The lumbermen logged off thousands of trees. This left only bare patches of ground where the grizzlies no longer could find food and shelter.

Some grizzlies were shot by "sportsmen" who wanted a bear skin rug in their den, or the head of a grizzly hanging on their living room wall. Some early settlers killed grizzlies to protect their families. Some grizzlies in New Mexico attacked and killed several hunters and gold miners.

A number of settlers slaughtered the bears for profit. They would sell both the hides and the meat. Because of humans, the grizzly population dropped off rapidly.

By 1900, not a single grizzly was left in Texas. By 1922, all the grizzlies had been killed off in California, Oregon, New Mexico, Colorado and Utah. Of the 900 or so grizzlies left in the lower United States, about 200 live in each of two national parks–Glacier and Yellowstone. A few exist in Washington and Idaho. Scientists now consider the grizzly a "threatened" species in the lower United States. This means that the population is dropping so fast the animal is in serious trouble.

Yellowstone National Park, home to the few remaining grizzlies in the United States.

Room to Roam

Grizzlies need wilderness in which to live. Wilderness is a natural area which has not been changed by humans. There are no houses, factories, roads, highways, cars, trucks, noise, or people. A wilderness has mountains, valleys, forests, lakes, streams and places where grizzlies could find food. It also has caves in which the bears could find shelter from storms. And it has hillsides where the bears could dig out dens for their winter sleep, or where the female could give birth to her young.

A grizzly bear on a hillside in Yellowstone Park.

Only a few good wilderness areas for grizzlies are left in the United States. Some of these are in Yellowstone National Park, Wyoming. Others are in Glacier National Park, Montana.

So what if these wilderness areas are not protected? What if roads and houses and factories are built in these areas? Then the grizzly will vanish from the lower United States.

Family

Grizzlies usually do not breed until they are six years old. The male mates with the female in summer. In late fall the pregnant female will dig out a den with her sharp claws. This may be in the side of a hill, just below a big rock, or under the roots of a large tree. She then enters the den and goes into a winter sleep. This is called hibernation.

During this time her heart rate slows down. Her body cools off. After several weeks she wakes up and gives birth to twin cubs. They are blind and naked at birth. Each weighs about one pound.

The cubs start nursing right away. By the end of one month their eyes are wide open. They will also have a soft covering of fur.

The mother and her cubs leave their den in early spring. The cubs start feeding on grasses and insects. The mother bear will rip open a bee hive so the cubs can lick the honey.

The mother also digs out ground squirrels from their burrows. The cubs then have a feast.

Grizzly cubs grow rapidly. By October they may weigh 40 pounds (18 kg)—40 times their birth weight! The mother will stay with her young for two to three years. Then they will be on their own.

A mother grizzly feeding her cubs.

Behavior

The area in which an animal lives is called its home range. It is where it travels while feeding, fighting, sleeping, breeding and taking shelter from storms and the cold. Some grizzlies will wander more than 50 miles in search of food, mates or shelter. The average home range of the male is about 100 square miles (161 square km). The female's is somewhat less–about 30 square miles (40 square km).

Within its home range the grizzly sets up its feeding territory. Such a territory has just enough food to keep one bear healthy. The territory's owner will defend it against other grizzlies. If an unwelcome grizzly strays into the territory, a threatening growl by the owner often frightens the stranger away.

Grizzlies and brown bears are often "loners" that stay inside their home ranges and territories. But in some cases they form groups. The mother bear and her young will travel together for up to two years before they separate. More than a dozen grizzlies or browns might gather where food is abundant, like a blackberry patch. Or they may gather where many deer are lying in the snow, dead from starvation, or where the salmon fishing is great. A group of at least 60 brown bears have been seen catching salmon on the McNeil River in Alaska.

Grizzlies and brown bears are usually quite peaceful. But sometimes they will fight. And their fights may be fierce. They might maul, rip and bite. One bear might even be killed.

Brown bears fighting for territory, McNeil River, Alaska.

Grizzly bears may fight to defend a territory that they set up in their home range. They may fight for a mate. This takes place during late summer or fall. The bear that loses the fight will hurry off in search of a mate elsewhere.

Grizzlies and brown bears also will fight over food. When fishing for salmon they will fight for the best place to fish. It may be a rock in the middle of the river. Usually the largest and oldest male bear wins all the fights and gets the best spot.

Brown bears fighting.

What Do Grizzlies Eat?

It takes a lot of food to fill the stomach of a hungry 800-pound (363-kg) grizzly bear. It eats a lot of plants. Surprisingly, grizzlies eat grass just like a cow. But they also feast on raspberries, blackberries, blueberries and other fruit when it ripens. It will dig out roots and chew on them. It has a great appetite for honey. A grizzly will

A grizzly bear foraging soapberries.

tear apart bee hives to get at the honey. It will fearlessly feed on both bees and wasps. The grizzly's thick fur protects it from their stings.

The grizzly is among the largest flesh-eating animals on Earth. But it often feeds on some of the world's smallest animals–the ants. It will tear open ant hills with its strong claws and lick up dozens of ants as they try to escape. It also will dig mice, chipmunks, squirrels, and woodchucks from their burrows.

Because of their great strength and quickness over short distances, grizzlies also eat much larger animals. One swipe of the grizzly's front paw can kill a deer, big horn sheep, mountain goat, or moose. It can easily overtake a black bear and kill it within seconds.

Alaskan brown bears catching salmon.

Buffalo were plentiful in the last century on the Great Plains. Some of them wound up as a meal. The grizzly is the only animal in the United States that could run down and kill a buffalo.

A brown bear feasting on a salmon.

The power of a full-grown grizzly is amazing. There are few animals that could drag a dead horse very far. One scientist watched a grizzly drag a horse 90 yards (82 m) before stopping to feed on it. Grizzlies will often eat animals such as birds, fox, woodchuck and deer that died from disease or were killed by cars.

In Alaska, there are many salmon streams and rivers. In late summer, the salmon swim up these waters to lay eggs. Some grizzlies wait on the bank for a salmon to swim close. Then they make a big "bellyflop" into the water and grab the big fish with their powerful jaws.

Other bears wade into the river until only their head and back stick out. They wait patiently in the rushing river as they look downstream. Then, when a salmon swims nearby, they lunge for it. Sometimes they miss. But not very often.

Attacks on Humans

The grizzly bear and brown bear are amazing animals. They have captured the interest of millions of Americans. In most cases they are perfectly harmless. However, they will attack humans. Usually this happens when they are surprised while looking for food. Or a mother bear might attack to protect her cubs.

In 1967, two young women hiked into the wilderness country of Glacier National Park in Montana. At nightfall, they pitched their tents and went to sleep. They never got out of those tents alive. A grizzly tore open their tent and killed them. This tragedy made news programs and newspaper headlines throughout America. People were horrified. Many demanded that all grizzlies in our national parks be destroyed.

The National Park Service promised to study the problem. The park officials found that only five people have been killed by grizzlies in our national parks in the past 100 years! Even more, only one of every one million park visitors is injured by a grizzly. This is a very low injury rate. Automobiles cause one injury for every 100 people. That's 10,000 times the rate of injuries caused by grizzlies.

The National Park Service decided not to kill off these interesting animals. Instead, it has tried to lower the chance of grizzly attacks by educating people. Visitors to Glacier and Yellowstone National Parks are warned immediately that grizzly bears live in the parks. Many trails leading to grizzly habitats have been closed to hikers. Campers have been warned not to throw food to the bears.

In the past some park visitors have thrown a grizzly a hamburger through an open car window so they could get a good picture. Such behavior is now forbidden. Food scraps left over

A brown bear with her cubs passing a tourist bus in Denali National Park, Alaska.

from picnicking must now be placed in garbage cans. These cans must be tightly closed so that grizzlies cannot sniff their way to them. If a grizzly is sighted near a campsite, park rangers sound a siren to warn visitors.

Finally, park rangers capture bears that have been a nuisance. Then they are either killed or hauled to back country far from the campsites. Since these actions were taken by the National Park Service, the rate of injury from grizzly attacks has dropped. Even better, not a single death from a grizzly has occurred in the United States since 1967.

From Cub to Grizzly Bear

When a baby grizzly is born it is blind and naked. But it can hear the moaning of the wind outside the den, the grunts of its mother, the squeals of the other cub, the calls of nearby birds and the buzzing of insects outside the cave. It can smell its mother and its twin, the grass, trees and flowers just outside the den, maybe even a mouse that scampers past the den. It can feel the warm bodies of its mother and the other cub, the rocks and soil on the floor of the den, and the cool breeze as it whisks past the den opening.

The cub is very weak. But it can move about. Much of the time it sucks its mother's milk. With each passing day it gets bigger and stronger.

By the time it is one month old it is no longer naked. Its body is covered with soft fur. Its eyes open. It can see its mother for the first time! It now knows what a grizzly looks like. And it will behave toward grizzlies in a very special way for the rest of its life.

A grizzly bear cub sitting in a meadow.

A brown bear with her cub, Alaskan Peninsula.

When spring comes the mother leads her cubs out of the den. Then they start looking for food. The bear cubs learn a lot about feeding from their mother. They watch her carefully when she lunges for squirrels or when she licks up ants.

When the cubs are three months old they no longer get milk from their mother. However, the mother grizzly makes sure they are well fed with grasses, fruits, berries, nuts and small animals. The cubs grow rapidly.

By October, the cubs weigh about 40 pounds (18 kg). The mother grizzly stays with her young until they are about three years old. Then they are on their own.

The female cub must take shelter from storms. She does this by crawling into a cave, or by crouching behind big rocks. This helps her stay fairly dry. The young female also must set

Brown bear cubs.

up a feeding territory. She will defend this territory against other grizzlies that stray into it. Defense of her territory is often not fierce. Just a few growls may chase the unwelcome grizzly away.

Sometimes the female grizzly may see a very strange-looking "animal"–a human being! She might hide in a thicket and simply stare at the human. She will be very curious as to

A mother brown bear showing her cubs how to catch fish.

what this "animal" is doing in her territory. But she will not attack–unless she is starving.

As she grows bigger she may catch and eat rabbits, squirrels, or even a young mountain goat. Sometimes food is scarce in the high country. She might get hungry and move down to the ranches and farms in the valley. Then she will stuff herself on apples, or beans and cabbages growing in gardens. She may even make a meal of a lamb or young pig.

Usually she finds enough food in her mountain wilderness. She may dig a woodchuck or fox out of its burrow and eat it. She may surprise a young deer and crush its skull with one sweep of her paw. After killing the deer she will tear off big chunks of flesh and stuff herself.

Maybe her territory will have a stretch of a river. When salmon are running upstream she may wade into the water and catch dozens of them.

When our grizzly bear is six years old she is ready to breed. After mating with a male, she will dig out a den. Then, as the cold weather comes, she will crawl slowly into her den and fall asleep. Though she no longer does any feeding, she will not starve. She will live for months on the fat that she stored up under her skin.

Some time later her babies will stir inside of her. She will wake up and soon give birth to twin cubs.

This is where our grizzly's life study began—and this is where it ends. It's an amazing story, don't you think?

A full grown Alaskan brown bear.

Glossary

Burrow   a hole in the ground dug by an animal for shelter or protection.

Carnivore   a meat-eating animal.

Den   a space dug out of a hillside where a bear can spend the winter.

Downstream   with the current of a stream.

Hibernate   to spend the winter sleeping or resting.

Livestock   farm animals (sheep, cattle, pigs, horses).

Loggers   a person who cuts down trees for a living.

Nurse   to give milk to a baby at the breast.

Range   the greatest distance at which an animal can operate or go.

Salmon   a large food fish with silvery scales and yellowish-pink flesh.

Species   a kind of plant or animal.

Pregnant   condition of a female which has a baby growing inside of her.

Territory   an area defended against other animals.

Wilderness   a part of nature which is unchanged by humans.

Bibliography

Encyclopedia Americana. Entry on Bears. Danbury, Conn.: Grolier, 1994.

Grzimek's Encyclopedia of Mammals. Volume 3. New York: McGraw-Hill, 1990.

Nowak, Ronald M. and John L. Paradiso. *Mammals of the World*. Baltimore: Johns Hopkins University Press, 1983.

Reid, Matt. *Road-building Can't Be Good for Grizzlies*. Bear News. Fall, 1994. p. 1.

Robinson, Wm. L. and Eric G. Bolden. *Wildlife Ecology and Management*. New York, Macmillan, 1984.

Van Gelder, Richard G. *Mammals of the National Parks*. Baltimore: Johns Hopkins University Press, 1982.

World Book Encyclopedia. Entry on Bears. Chicago: Field Enterprises, 1990.

Index

About the Author

Oliver S. Owen is a Professor Emeritus for the University of Wisconsin at Eau Claire. He is the coauthor of *Natural Resource Conservation: An Ecological Approach* (Macmillan, 1991). Dr. Owen has also authored *Eco-Solutions, Intro to Your Environment* (Abdo & Daughters, 1993), and the Lifewatch series (Abdo & Daughters, 1994). Dr. Owen has a Ph.D. in zoology from Cornell University.

To my grandson, Amati: May you grow up to always appreciate and love nature.
—Grandpa Ollie.